The Fried Rice Cookbook

Easy and Delicious Fried Rice Recipes from Around the World!

BY: Nancy Silverman

COPYRIGHT NOTICES

© **2019 Nancy Silverman All Rights Reserved**

Subject to the agreement and permission of the author, this Book, in part or in whole, may not be reproduced in any format. This includes but is not limited to electronically, in print, scanning or photocopying.

The opinions, guidelines and suggestions written here are solely those of the Author and are for information purposes only. Every possible measure has been taken by the Author to ensure accuracy but let the Reader be advised that they assume all risk when following information. The Author does not assume any risk in the case of damages, personally or commercially, in the case of misinterpretation or misunderstanding while following any part of the Book.

My Heartfelt Thanks and A Special Reward for Your Purchase!

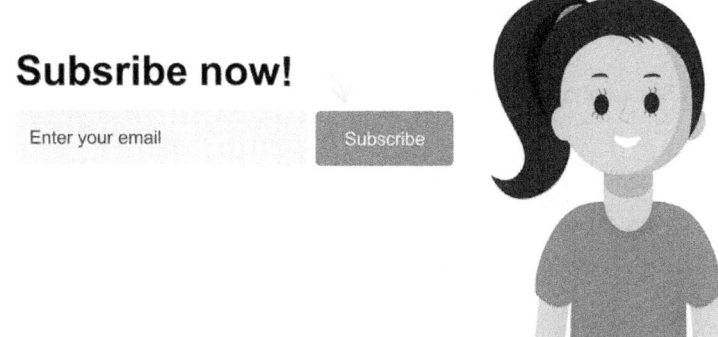

https://nancy.gr8.com

My heartfelt thanks at purchasing my book and I hope you enjoy it! As a special bonus, you will now be eligible to receive books absolutely free on a weekly basis! Get started by entering your email address in the box above to subscribe. A notification will be emailed to you of my free promotions, no purchase necessary! With little effort, you will be eligible for free and discounted books daily. In addition to this amazing gift, a reminder will be sent 1-2 days before the offer expires to remind you not to miss out. Enter now to start enjoying this special offer!

Table of Contents

(1) Spinach and Parmesan Fried Rice 6

(2) Cheesy Spicy Fried Rice 9

(3) Sausage and Veggie Fried Rice.................................... 12

(4) Fried Tomatoes Rice 16

(5) Lean Beef Fried Rice with Corn................................... 19

(6) Fried Rice with Hot Dogs.. 22

(7) Ground Beef and Broccoli Fried Rice.......................... 25

(8) Fried Rice with Sautéed Scallops 28

(9) Ham and Peas Fried White Rice.................................. 31

(10) Fried Rice with Bacon Bites and Dried Tomatoes 34

(11) Fried Shrimp and Pineapple on Rice.......................... 37

(12) Teriyaki Turkey Fried Rice... 41

(13) Fried Rice with Tofu Bites and Brussel Sprouts 44

(14) Olives and Salmon Fried Rice..................................... 47

(15) Cashews and Chicken on Fried Rice............................ 50

(16) Tuna on Top of Fried Rice... 53

(17) Sweet and Sour Fried Rice Idea 56

(18) Coconut Milk and Fried Rice Together...................... 59

(19) Refreshing Lime Fried Rice....................................... 62

(20) Fried Rice with Some Sweetness............................... 65

(21) Kale and Pork Fried Rice... 68

(22) Yummy Fried Rice Cakes.. 71

(23) Yellow Fried Rice with A Fried Egg 74

(24) The Perfect Mexican Fried Rice Idea......................... 76

(25) Mushrooms, Beans and Fried Rice 79

About the Author.. 82

Author's Afterthoughts... 84

(1) Spinach and Parmesan Fried Rice

Fried rice does not have to be loaded with meat, as you learned along the way. If there is one thing to remember from his book, remember this: you can make your fried rice with almost any ingredients or food items you love, it's all about frying it with the right combination of spices/ingredients that will taste good together.

Serving Size: 3-6

Total Prep Time: 30-45 minutes

Ingredient List:

- 3 cups cooked basmati rice
- 4 cups fresh baby spinach leaves
- 1 cup shredded Parmesan cheese
- 2 minced garlic cloves
- ½ chopped red onion
- 3 Tbsps. pesto sauce (homemade or store bought, your favorite is just fine)
- 2 Tbsps. olive oil
- ¼ cup roasted pine nuts
- Salt, black pepper

Instructions:

- For each recipe, I will start by saying that you can really choose the rice you prefer: brown rice, white rice, Basmati rice, Jasmine rice, Arborio rice, black rice or any other rice you may like to try.
- Next, heat the olive oil in a large skillet, or a wok if you own one.
- Cook the garlic and onion for 5 minutes.
- Add the spinach and cook another 3 minutes.
- Add the cooked rice, the pine nuts, the pesto sauce and Parmesan cheese.
- Finally, mix all the ingredients together and taste before serving, adjust the seasonings if needed.
- I always keep a few extra pine nuts to decorate the rice once serving.

(2) Cheesy Spicy Fried Rice

The combination of the spices with the melted cheese will make you wish you knew about this recipe a long time ago. It's never too late! Enjoy this recipe to its fullest and don't ever look back at what you have been missing on for years.

Serving Size: 3-6

Total Prep Time: 30-45 minutes

Ingredient List:

- 2 cups shredded low fat Mozzarella cheese
- 3 cups cooked white rice
- ¼ cup spicy clam juice
- 2 large eggs
- 1 Tablespoon red pepper flakes
- ½ teaspoon black pepper
- ½ teaspoon cayenne pepper
- Salt

Instructions:

- Once your white rice is cooked, heat a large skillet and add some cooking oil.
- Add the rice, all seasonings and fry for 5 minutes.
- Add the clam juice and make room to fry the eggs also.
- Once the eggs are fried, mix all ingredients together and finally add the cheese.
- Mix again and continue cooking until the cheese has melted.
- Serve warm.

(3) Sausage and Veggie Fried Rice

Let's start this recipe book with our first awesome recipe: sausage and veggie fried rice. You might wonder what type of sausages are the best to use. My answer would actually be the kind you prefer. We will show you a recipe with hot dogs later, so maybe for this one you could choose bratwurst or Italian sausage? Let's see what we picked!

Serving Size: 4

Total Prep Time: 40 minutes

Ingredient List:

- ½ pound grounded Italian turkey sausage
- 1 cup sweet peas
- 1 large egg
- 2 minced green onions
- 1 diced yellow squash
- 1 minced clove garlic
- 2 Tbsps. olive oil
- 1 Tablespoon chili powder
- ½ teaspoon cumin
- 3 cups cooked rice of your choice

Instructions:

- For each recipe, I will start by saying that you can really choose the rice you prefer: brown rice, white rice, Basmati rice, Jasmine rice, Arborio rice, black rice or any other rice you may like to try.
- Next, heat the olive oil in a large skillet, or a wok if you own one.
- Start by cooking the Italian sausage for 15 minutes or so, stirring so it stays crumbly.
- When the sausage is done, remove some of the fat and add the onions, garlic, and diced squash, and all seasonings.
- Stir and cook for an additional 5 minutes.
- Then add the cooked rice and make a hole in the middle of the pan to crack the egg and fry it until done.

- Finally, mix all the ingredients together again and taste before serving, adjust the seasonings if needed.

(4) Fried Tomatoes Rice

Now, this reminds me somewhat of my childhood. It was not our favorite dish, by any means, but my mom used to make fried rice after cooking the rice originally with tomato juice instead of plain water. This is how we started this recipe and stay tuned to learn how we finish it.

Serving Size: 3-6

Total Prep Time: 30-45 minutes

Ingredient List:

- 4 cups tomato juice
- 2 cups uncooked white rice
- ½ can diced seasoned diced tomatoes
- 1 diced green bell pepper
- ½ chopped sweet onion
- ½ teaspoon curry powder
- 1 teaspoon cayenne pepper
- Salt, black pepper
- Cooking oil

Instructions:

- For this recipe, make sure you cook your rice in tomato juice instead of water.
- In a skillet, heat the oil and cook the pepper and onions for 5 minutes.
- Add the diced tomatoes next along with the cooked tomato rice and all seasonings.
- Use a wooden spoon to continue cooking and frying the rice for another 10-12 minutes.
- Enjoy!

(5) Lean Beef Fried Rice with Corn

Many beef cuts are appropriate for stir fry recipes such as sirloin, tenderloin, top loin and of course rib eye. Cut the beef in trips or cubes and stir way. Adding corn will throw many off, maybe you used to add broccoli florets, but corn will add that sweet touch.

Serving Size: 4

Total Prep Time: 40 minutes

Ingredient List:

- ½ pound piece tenderloin or ribeye steak strips
- 1 Tablespoon apple cider vinegar
- 1 Tablespoon cornstarch
- 3 Tbsps. soy sauce
- 1 fresh diced, peeled and pitted avocado
- 1 Tablespoon lemon juice
- 2 medium eggs
- 3 cups cooked brown rice
- 2 Tbsps. avocado oil
- Salt, black pepper

Instructions:

- For each recipe, I will start by saying that you can really choose the rice you prefer: brown rice, white rice, Basmati rice, Jasmine rice, Arborio rice, black rice or any other rice you may like to try.
- Next, heat the avocado oil in a large skillet, or a wok if you own one.
- Cook the beef for 5 minutes. Meanwhile, in a small bowl, mix the soy sauce, lemon juice, salt, pepper, vinegar and cornstarch.
- Add to the sauce to the meat and make room, then fry the eggs in the pan as well.
- Finally, add the cooked rice and mix again to let it fry for 10 minutes.
- When done, serve with diced, fresh avocado pieces on top.

(6) Fried Rice with Hot Dogs

Let's keep things very simple. You have leftover grilled or boiled hot dogs from last night's party? Then let's make some fried rice including these tasty sausages so there is no waste and some happy faces instead!

Serving Size: 3-6

Total Prep Time: 30-45 minutes

Ingredient List:

- 6 hot dogs (I prefer beef)
- 1 finely chopped leek
- 1 cup fresh cut trimmed green beans
- 1 diced red bell pepper
- 3 cups cooked white rice
- 3 Tbsps. olive oil
- ½ cup white eggs
- 3 Tbsps. ketchup
- ½ teaspoon cayenne pepper
- ½ teaspoon black pepper
- 1 teaspoon garlic powder
- 1 teaspoon onion powder

Instructions:

- Chop the hot digs in small slices and set aside.
- Heat the oil in a skillet, add the veggies, hot dogs and cook 10 minutes.
- Add the cooked rice and all seasonings, along with the ketchup. Mix well and make room to fry the eggs.
- Once the eggs are cooked, mix again and taste before serving, adjusting the seasonings if needed.

(7) Ground Beef and Broccoli Fried Rice

Ground beef is not only good in tacos, it is also awesome added to fried rice along with broccoli and other veggies if you desire. This is the beauty of fried rice recipes; they can be made with a variety of meats and matched with the right seasonings per the one chosen.

Serving Size: 3-6

Total Prep Time: 30-45 minutes

Ingredient List:

- 1 pound lean ground beef
- 3 cups cooked basmati rice
- 1 small chopped yellow onion
- 1 large chopped peeled carrot
- 1 cup diced fresh tomatoes
- 2 chopped celery stalks
- ½ cup salsa Verde
- 2 medium eggs
- 2 Tbsps. olive oil
- 1 Tablespoon chili powder
- ½ teaspoon garlic powder
- Salt, black pepper

Instructions:

- For each recipe, I will start by saying that you really can choose the rice you prefer: brow rice, white rice, Basmati rice, Jasmine rice, Arborio rice, black rice or any other rice you may like to try.
- Next, heat the olive oil in a large skillet, or a wok if you own one.
- Add the ground meat and cook until done, remove the excess fat.
- Add the veggies (except tomatoes), the cooked rice, and cook another 6-7 minutes.
- Make room to fry the eggs, season everything with salt, pepper, garlic powder, chili powder, and when eggs are done, stir to mix all the ingredients together.
- Serve with some salsa Verde on top and fresh diced tomatoes.

(8) Fried Rice with Sautéed Scallops

Now, this might be fancier than the fried rice you are used to; but fancy, and for-special-occasion recipes are good to have handy. Pour yourself a nice glass of wine on a Saturday night and fully enjoy your scallops served on rice.

Serving Size: 3-6

Total Prep Time: 30-45 minutes

Ingredient List:

- ½ pound bay scallops
- 3 cups cooked brown rice
- 1 cup chopped yellow onion
- 1 Tablespoon minced garlic
- 2 Tbsps. olive oil
- 2 large eggs
- 2 Tbsps. chopped fresh parsley
- 2 Tbsps. fresh chopped chives

Instructions:

- Clean and prepare your small bay scallops.
- Heat the oil in the skillet and start frying the scallops along with the garlic, onion and herbs, for about 10 minutes.
- Add the cooked rice and make room to fry the eggs in the pan.
- Next, heat the olive oil in a large skillet, or a wok if you own one.
- Finally, mix all the ingredients together again and taste before serving, adjust the seasonings if needed.
- You can even add a little white wine when you first cook the scallops if you like.

(9) Ham and Peas Fried White Rice

Cooked ham can be added to casseroles, dishes and sides, including fried rice. If you can purchase some fresh sweet peas, good for you, if not, you could use the frozen ones to add to the rice and then follow the suggested seasonings as well.

Serving Size: 3-6

Total Prep Time: 30-45 minutes

Ingredient List:

- 1 ½ cup cooked diced ham
- 1 cup sweet peas
- 1 cup diced carrots
- 3 cups cooked white rice
- 2 Tbsps. sesame oil
- 2 Tbsps. sesame seeds
- 1 Tablespoon minced garlic
- 1 Tablespoon rice vinegar
- 1 Tablespoon brown sugar
- 1 Tablespoon soy sauce

Instructions:

- For each recipe, I will start by saying that you can really choose the rice you prefer: brown rice, white rice, Basmati rice, Jasmine rice, Arborio rice, black rice or any other rice you may like to try.
- Next, heat the sesame oil in a large skillet, or a wok if you own one.
- Add the sesame seeds, garlic, vinegar, brown sugar and soy sauce, and mix well in the pan.
- Add the ham and veggies and let them caramelize a little.
- Finally, add the cooked rice and mix well.

(10) Fried Rice with Bacon Bites and Dried Tomatoes

Bacon is a food staple. You should keep bacon almost year-round in your fridge or freezer. Then, you can improvise and make a delicious fried rice like this one at the last minute, and totally blow away anyone who would taste it. I have to say that the sundried tomatoes also mix nicely with the bacon.

Serving Size: 3-6

Total Prep Time: 30-45 minutes

Ingredient List:

- ½ cup chopped sundried tomatoes
- 1 cup crumbled turkey bacon
- 1 cup fresh diced tomatoes
- 1 cup crumbled Feta cheese
- 3 cups Jasmine rice
- 2 Tbsps. walnut oil
- ¼ cup chopped walnuts
- 1 Tablespoon chopped fresh oregano
- Salt, black pepper

Instructions:

- I encourage you to use Jasmine rice for this one; you will not regret your choice.
- Fry the walnut oil in the skillet, add the diced tomatoes, all seasonings and sundried tomatoes.
- A few minutes later, add the cooked bacon, rice and walnuts.
- Stir well with a wooden spoon, so everything gets mixed.
- Serve with chopped fresh parsley on top if you like.

(11) Fried Shrimp and Pineapple on Rice

Nothing like fried shrimp in fried rice, it's as close to heaven as you can get in once dish! But wait a minute, if you decide to add some fresh diced pineapple to it, you might get even closer, as to some of us, this dish is "to die for"!

Serving Size: 3-6

Total Prep Time: 30-45 minutes

Ingredient List:

- ½ pound small shrimp (deveined, peeled and cleaned)
- 1 cup panko breadcrumbs
- 1 large egg
- 3 Tbsps. beer (any kind is fine)
- ½ teaspoon garlic powder
- Salt, pepper
- 1 cup fresh diced pineapple
- 1 cup bean sprouts
- 2 Tbsps. hoisin sauce
- 2 Tbsps. olive oil
- Salt, black pepper

Instructions:

- For each recipe, I will start by saying that you can really choose the rice you prefer: brown rice, white rice, Basmati rice, Jasmine rice, Arborio rice, black rice or any other rice you may like to try.
- Next, let's make the fried shrimp.
- Prepare the batter by mixing in bowl the panko crumbs, garlic powder, salt, pepper. In a second bowl, mix the egg and beer.
- Take each shrimp individually and bread it before cooking it in hot oil in your skillet.
- Once the shrimp are done, remove and let the excess fat get absorbed in paper towels.

- Add a little more oil, the hoisin sauce and seasonings to the skillet, and cook the beans sprouts, diced pineapple for a few minutes with the eggs.
- Finally add the cooked rice, mix well and adjust seasonings if needed.

(12) Teriyaki Turkey Fried Rice

Soy sauce or teriyaki sauce are both equally used and equally yummy in fried rice. This recipe happens to call for teriyaki sauce and the carrots marry well with that taste. Add some turkey, or chicken, and you are all set!

Serving Size: 3-6

Total Prep Time: 30-45 minutes

Ingredient List:

- 2 cups cooked shredded turkey
- 3 cups cooked brown rice
- 2 cups Macedonia veggies (frozen mix of diced carrots, peas and corn is great)
- 2 cups sliced fresh mushrooms
- 1 Tablespoon minced garlic
- ¼ chopped red onion
- 5 Tbsps. teriyaki sauce
- 2 Tbsps. sesame oil
- Salt, black pepper

Instructions:

- For each recipe, I will start by saying that you can really choose the rice you prefer: brown rice, white rice, Basmati rice, Jasmine rice, Arborio rice, black rice or any other rice you may like to try.
- Mix the oil, teriyaki sauce, and all seasonings in a bowl.
- Heat the oil mixture in a skillet and cook the mushrooms, garlic and onions for 5 minutes.
- Add the cooked turkey, cooked rice and other veggies.
- Continue frying, stirring often for another 10-15 minutes.
- Serve warm.

(13) Fried Rice with Tofu Bites and Brussel Sprouts

Here is a dish that is perfectly acceptable for anyone, including my vegetarian friends! I love the taste of shredded Brussels sprouts in many casseroles, salads, and now in fried rice too. The tofu, if marinated and sautéed to perfection will complete this fried rice recipe just as expected

Serving Size: 3-6

Total Prep Time: 30-45 minutes.

Ingredient List:

- 1 large tofu block (cubed or strips)
- 3 cups cooked brown rice
- ½ pound shredded Brussel sprouts
- 2 tablespoons Worcestershire sauce
- 3 tablespoons olive oil
- 1 Tablespoon minced garlic
- 1 Tablespoon minced ginger
- Salt, black pepper
- 2 minced green onions

Instructions:

- For each recipe, I will start by saying that you can really choose the rice you prefer: brown rice, white rice, Basmati rice, Jasmine rice, Arborio rice, black rice or any other rice you may like to try.
- First, drain the tofu from the package and cut in cubes or strips.
- Heat the olive oil and add the Worcestershire sauce, start cooking the tofu for 10 minutes.
- Add the garlic, ginger and green onions, and cook for another for 5 minutes.
- Finally, add the cooked rice, mix all the ingredients together again and taste before serving, adjust the seasonings if needed.

(14) Olives and Salmon Fried Rice

Another way to serve your salmon is to use the fried rice excuse. Not a bad thought at all I must say, because I have tasted it and enjoyed it many times so far. If you are not an olives lover, you could substitute with other ingredients such as capers or roasted peppers.

Serving Size: 3-6

Total Prep Time: 30-45 minutes

Ingredient List:

- 2 large cooked salmon filets
- 2 tablespoons lemon juice
- ¼ cup white dry wine
- 2 tablespoons chopped fresh cilantro
- 3 cups cooked brown rice
- 2 tablespoons avocado oil
- ¼ cup mixed, chopped or sliced olives (black and green, or your favorite kind)

Instructions:

- You should use brown rice with this recipe, I personally prefer it.
- Heat avocado oil and cook the cilantro with a little lemon juice, wine in the skillet first.
- Add the salmon filets that you have cut in small pieces ahead of time.
- Add the cooked rice and olives.
- Finally, mix all the ingredients together again and taste before serving, adjusting the seasonings if needed.
- Serve with lemon wedges if you can.

(15) Cashews and Chicken on Fried Rice

I am a big nuts fan. My kids will even say that sometimes I might be a little nuts!!!! Joking aside, cashews are by far my favorite nuts and to have a dish that allows me to add as much or as little as I want is awesome. Most of the time I will make this dish with chicken, but if you have pork to cook, that's awesome as well.

Serving Size: 3-6

Total Prep Time: 30-45 minutes

Ingredient List:

- 3 cups steamed broccoli floret
- ¾ cup chopped roasted cashews
- 3 cups cooked Jasmine rice
- 2 Tbsps. olive oil
- 1 Tablespoon rice vinegar
- 1 Tablespoon green chilies
- 1 cup sweet corn
- Salt, black pepper
- ½ teaspoon dried thyme

Instructions:

- For each recipe, I will start by saying that you can really choose the rice you prefer: brown rice, white rice, Basmati rice, Jasmine rice, Arborio rice, black rice or any other rice you may like to try.
- In a bowl, mix the green chilies, thyme, salt, pepper, olive oil and vinegar.
- Start heating this mixture in the skillet and add the precooked broccoli, cashews, corn and rice. Let it all fry together for 10-12 minutes.
- Finally, mix all the ingredients together again and taste before serving, adjusting the seasonings if needed.

(16) Tuna on Top of Fried Rice

Let's make some fried rice cakes topped with tuna. Sounds really complicated? No, not at all, and please don't think it will be for a second. We will walk you through the recipe and all the ingredients are, as always, easily found in your local grocery store.

Serving Size: 3-6

Total Prep Time: 30-45 minutes

Ingredient List:

- 2 large white tuna cans in oil (well drained)
- 2 Tbsps. mayonnaise
- 4 cups cooked rice
- 1 Tablespoon garlic powder
- 1 Tablespoon onion powder
- ¼ cup vegetable broth
- 1 Tablespoon lemon juice
- 1 Tablespoon olive oil
- 1 cup sweet corn
- 2 minced green onions
- Salt, black pepper

Instructions:

- For each recipe, I will start by saying that you can really choose the rice you prefer: brown rice, white rice, Basmati rice, Jasmine rice, Arborio rice, black rice or any other rice you may like to try.
- Make the rice first by frying together the oil, green onions, all seasonings, lemon juice, and corn.
- Add the cooked rice and the vegetables broth and let it fry for another 10 minutes.
- Meanwhile, mix the mayonnaise with the tuna in the bowl, adding some salt and black pepper.
- Serve on a bed of fried rice and top it off with generous portion of the tuna salad.

(17) Sweet and Sour Fried Rice Idea

What makes successful or good sweet and sour fried rice? I like the taste of pineapple mixed with artichokes in this particular recipe. If you don't like artichoke, please remove it from the list and add any other veggie or fruit of your choice.

Serving Size: 3-6

Total Prep Time: 30-45 minutes

Ingredient List:

- 3 cups cooked Basmati rice
- 1 cup diced fresh pineapple
- 1 cup marinated chopped artichoke
- 1 chopped red bell pepper
- 1 Tablespoon soy sauce
- 3 Tbsps. ketchup or chili sauce
- 4 Tbsps. brown sugar
- 4 Tbsps. rice vinegar
- 2 Tbsps. water
- 1 Tablespoon cornstarch

Instructions:

- For each recipe, I will start by saying that you can really choose the rice you prefer: brown rice, white rice, Basmati rice, Jasmine rice, Arborio rice, black rice or any other rice you may like to try.
- Make the sweet and sour sauce by mixing together the cornstarch, water, vinegar, brown sugar and ketchup in small pot, on medium heat.
- Add the veggies and fruits to a skillet with a little oil and cook for 5 minutes.
- Pour in the sweet and sour sauce and the cooked rice and continue.
- Finally, mix all the ingredients together again and taste before serving, adjust the seasonings as needed.

(18) Coconut Milk and Fried Rice Together

Coconut milk and fried rice mix well together. It gives a very special twist to the fried rice and you can add some different meats to match it with such as pork, chicken, turkey or even tofu. Enjoy!

Serving Size: 3-6

Total Prep Time: 30-45 minutes

Ingredient List:

- 3 cups cooked basmati rice
- ½ can coconut milk with the cream found on top
- 1 Tablespoon Curry powder
- Salt, black pepper
- Pinch of cumin
- 2 cups cooked broccoli florets
- 2 cups cooked cauliflower florets
- 1 can rinsed and drained white beans

Instructions:

- For each recipe, I will start by saying that you can really choose the rice you prefer: brown rice, white rice, Basmati rice, Jasmine rice, Arborio rice, black rice or any other rice you may like to try.
- In a skillet, mix the coconut milk with the curry powder and all the other seasonings. Add the cooked veggies, beans and cooked rice.
- Finally, mix all the ingredients together again and taste before serving, adjusting the seasonings if needed.
- You can sprinkle a few coconut flakes on top of this fried rice when serving if you wish.

(19) Refreshing Lime Fried Rice

Lime and coconut seem to go together, but in this case, I am talking about lime and cucumbers. That's right, this fried rice will be super refreshing and unique and you will be asked for the recipe when serving it to your friends, because it is so different.

Serving Size: 3-6

Total Prep Time: 30-45 minutes

Ingredient List:

- 3 cups cooked white rice
- 2 cups cooked shredded chicken
- 2 Tbsps. avocado oil
- 3 Tbsps. lime juice
- 1 Tablespoon lime zest
- 1 diced seedless cucumber
- 1 cup sweet peas
- Salt, black pepper
- ½ teaspoon ground cumin
- ½ teaspoon ground sage

Instructions:

- For each recipe, I will start by saying that you can really choose the rice you prefer: brown rice, white rice, Basmati rice, Jasmine rice, Arborio rice, black rice or any other rice you may like to try.
- In a bowl, mix the oil, lime juice, lime zest, cumin, sage, salt and pepper.
- Heat this oil mixture in the skillet and add the diced cucumber and sweet peas as well as the rice and the cooked chicken.
- Let all the ingredients fry together for 10-15 minutes, stir often.

(20) Fried Rice with Some Sweetness

Because you are preparing fried rice, that does not mean it must be super salty, saucy or even seasoned with soy sauce, or other very tasty sauces. It can contain sweet ingredients and add-ons that make the fried rice more like desert rice. Not that you would really serve it as a desert, but possibly with a grilled meat or even with a spicy chicken dish to tone down the spices of the overall dish.

Serving Size: 3-6

Total Prep Time: 30-45 minutes

Ingredient List:

- 3 cups cooked brown rice
- ½ cup golden dried raisins
- ¼ cup sliced almonds
- ¼ cup orange juice
- 1 Tablespoon orange zest
- 2 Tbsps. almond milk
- 1 Tablespoon coconut oil
- 2 Tbsps. lemon juice
- ½ teaspoon ground nutmeg
- ½ teaspoon ground cinnamon

Instructions:

- For each recipe, I will start by saying that you can really choose the rice you prefer: brown rice, white rice, Basmati rice, Jasmine rice, Arborio rice, black rice or any other rice you may like to try.
- In a bowl, mix the juices, oil, milk, orange zest, spices.
- Heat that mixture in the skillet and add the cooked rice, dried raisins and almonds.
- Make sure to combine all the ingredients with a wooden spoon and fry this rice for another 10-12 minutes.
- Taste and serve!

(21) Kale and Pork Fried Rice

Kale is a super food, a super veggie, so let's start using it in as many dishes as possible. I am not sure if you ever thought about using it in fried rice, but honestly, why wouldn't we? It mixes really well with other ingredients and the slight bitterness of this type of green disappears when rightly seasoned.

Serving Size: 3-6

Total Prep Time: 30-45 minutes

Ingredient List:

- 3 cups chopped kale leaves
- 1 large red bell pepper cut in strips
- 1 medium size zucchini cut in strips
- ½ chopped red onion
- 1 tablespoon minced garlic
- ½ pound pork tenderloin cut in strips
- 3 cups cooked brown rice
- 2 Tbsps. teriyaki sauce
- 2 Tbsps. honey
- 1 Tablespoon white balsamic vinegar
- 4 Tbsps. sesame oil
- Salt, black pepper
- Pinch red pepper flakes

Instructions:

- For each recipe, I will start by saying that you can really choose the rice you prefer: brown rice, white rice, Basmati rice, Jasmine rice, Arborio rice, black rice or any other rice you may like to try.
- Next, heat a tablespoon of sesame oil and cook the pork strips for 10 minutes.
- Add all the veggies and garlic, as well as more oil, and cook for another 5 minutes.
- In a bowl, mix the teriyaki sauce, honey, vinegar and seasonings and dump in the skillet before adding the cooked rice.
- Mix well and fry another 10 minutes.
- I usually eat this fried rice with a little added hot sauce.

(22) Yummy Fried Rice Cakes

Let's make some fried rice cakes like you would tuna cakes or even crab cakes. These can be served easily as an appetizer or as a side dish to a nice fresh garden salad. They also freeze really well.

Serving Size: 3-6

Total Prep Time: 30-45 minutes

Ingredient List:

- 4 cups cooked white rice
- 2 large eggs
- ½ cup panko crumbs
- 2 minced green onions
- 1 Tablespoon lime juice
- 1 Tablespoon lime zest
- 2 Tbsps. Chopped fresh parsley
- 1 Tablespoon chili powder
- Salt, black pepper

Instructions:

- You are not making fried rice per say, but rice cakes.
- So, let's start by mixing all ingredients in a large bowl, except the oil.
- Form about 8 patties or more if you prefer them smaller.
- Heat the cooking oil of your choice in a large skillet and fry the rice cakes 10 minutes on each side.
- Enjoy with your favorite dipping sauce.

(23) Yellow Fried Rice with A Fried Egg

Are you ready to eat a fried rice recipe for breakfast? What if I told you it would be served with a fried egg on top, would that make any difference? What if I told you that you can have a fried egg at any meal, it does not matter?

Serving Size: 3-6

Total Prep Time: 30-45 minutes

Ingredient List:

- 1 large egg per serving, so about 4
- Olive oil
- 3 cups cooked yellow rice (usually I buy it in bag and the spices are always mixed in)
- 4 Tbsps. sour cream
- Handful fresh parsley when serving
- Salt, black pepper

Instructions:

- For this recipe, as specified, I recommend the yellow rice.
- Heat olive oil in a large skillet and fry 4 eggs sunny side up, season them with salt and pepper.
- When serving, lay a cup of yellow rice, a fried egg on top, a little sour cream and some fresh parsley to decorate.

(24) The Perfect Mexican Fried Rice Idea

No matter what Nationality you are, everyone likes a little Mexican influence in their dish once in a while. So, although we are "typically" used to associating fried rice with Chinese or Japanese cuisine, let's turn things around and add some Mexican spices and ingredients to make it our own here.

Serving Size: 3-6

Total Prep Time: 30-45 minutes

Ingredient List:

- 2 Tbsps. olive oil
- 4 cups cooked Arborio rice
- 1 can seasoned black beans (rinsed and well drained)
- ½ cup chunky salsa
- ½ cup tomato sauce
- 1 cup sweet corn
- 1 small chopped yellow onion
- 2 Tbsps. chopped fresh cilantro
- ½ envelop taco seasonings
- Salt and pepper if necessary

Instructions:

- For each recipe, I will start by saying that you can really choose the rice you prefer: brown rice, white rice, Basmati rice, Jasmine rice, Arborio rice, black rice or any other rice you may like to try.
- Now, heat the olive oil in a large skillet, cook the onion and cilantro for a few minutes.
- Add the beans, salsa, cooked rice, corn, tomato sauce and all seasonings.
- Stir very well so all the ingredients get mixed.
- Continue cooking for 10 minutes and serve.

(25) Mushrooms, Beans and Fried Rice

Mushrooms are one of my family's favorite veggies. Combined with garlic and other veggies it can add all the awesomeness necessary to fried rice. In this recipe, we also decided to include black beans, to add some extra proteins.

Serving Size: 3-6

Total Prep Time: 30-45 minutes

Ingredient List:

- 4 slices fresh mushrooms
- 1 can red kidney (well rinsed and drained)
- 1 cup diced marinated artichoke
- 2 Tbsps. olive oil
- ½ teaspoon cumin
- ½ teaspoon garlic salt
- ½ teaspoon onion powder
- ½ teaspoon cayenne pepper
- ½ teaspoon black pepper
- 4 cups cooked brown rice

Instructions:

- For each recipe, I will start by saying that you can really choose the rice you prefer: brown rice, white rice, Basmati rice, Jasmine rice, Arborio rice, black rice or any other rice you may like to try.
- Next, heat the olive oil in a large skillet, or a wok if you own one.
- Cook the mushrooms first for 10 minutes. Add all the other ingredients, including the rice. Stir often to make sure all the seasonings mix well.
- Taste, adjust as needed, and serve.

About the Author

Nancy Silverman is an accomplished chef from Essex, Vermont. Armed with her degree in Nutrition and Food Sciences from the University of Vermont, Nancy has excelled at creating e-books that contain healthy and delicious meals that anyone can make and everyone can enjoy. She improved her cooking skills at the New England Culinary Institute in Montpelier Vermont and she has been working at perfecting her culinary style since graduation. She claims that her life's work is always a work in progress and she only hopes to be an inspiration to aspiring chefs everywhere.

Her greatest joy is cooking in her modern kitchen with her family and creating inspiring and delicious meals. She often says that she has perfected her signature dishes based on her family's critique of each and every one.

Nancy has her own catering company and has also been fortunate enough to be head chef at some of Vermont's most exclusive restaurants. When a friend suggested she share some of her outstanding signature dishes, she decided to add cookbook author to her repertoire of personal achievements. Being a technological savvy woman, she felt the e-book realm would be a better fit and soon she had her first cookbook available online. As of today, Nancy has sold over 1,000 e-books and has shared her culinary experiences and brilliant recipes with people from all over the world! She plans on expanding into self-help books and dietary cookbooks, so stayed tuned!

Author's Afterthoughts

Thank you for making the decision to invest in one of my cookbooks! I cherish all my readers and hope you find joy in preparing these meals as I have.

There are so many books available and I am truly grateful that you decided to buy this one and follow it from beginning to end.

I love hearing from my readers on what they thought of this book and any value they received from reading it. As a personal favor, I would appreciate any feedback you can give in the form of a review on Amazon and please be honest! This kind of support will help others make an informed choice on and will help me tremendously in producing the best quality books possible.

My most heartfelt thanks,

Nancy Silverman

If you're interested in more of my books, be sure to follow my author page on Amazon (can be found on the link Bellow) or scan the QR-Code.

https://www.amazon.com/author/nancy-silverman

Printed in Great Britain
by Amazon

24809042R10051